#SELLOUT

How a Great Experience Can Help You *#SellOut* of Your Product

BY AWARD-WINNING TRAINER

KORY ANGELIN

outskirts
press

Dedication

This book is dedicated to my beautiful Mother. A woman who was not afraid of anything in this world, especially speaking her mind. A woman whose strength and character I could only hope to inherit. A woman whose bravery throughout her life is an inspiration to everyone who met her. I could not have achieved anything in life without your guidance, love and wisdom. Dawn, Kameron and myself know you are looking down on us and smiling.

Table of Contents

Preface

55% OF THE PEOPLE MAKING THEIR LIVING IN SALES DON'T HAVE THE RIGHT SKILLS TO BE SUCCESSFUL. -THEBREVITGROUP

Everyone is in the sales business. Whether you sell a product, service or just trying to sell your friend on the idea of going to your favorite restaurant. The ability, however, to be great at sales requires that you understand the philosophy behind it.

Why does a customer buy a product or service? Why does a customer say no to a sale? In order for you to understand why a customer buys a product or service, you need to understand what is most important to the customer. In other words, everyone is willing to spend money on something that is of value to him or her. The question is, how well of a job did you do in presenting your product or service and, more importantly, did you build value in it?

In order for you to be better at sales, you need to understand how not to sell. Yes I know, you think it is crazy that you just purchased a book on how to be great at sales and I am actually going to teach you how not to sell. What I mean by this is that most sales interactions are nothing more than an attempt at a transaction based on price. The magic in sales really comes down to having the ability to create a relationship with the guest and not worrying about what you have to sell. Building rapport with a guest is the most critical component in sales and, if done correctly, will most likely lead to a sale. This component, however, is most often overlooked. Most people in sales lack the ability or effort to try and connect with a customer. If you don't believe me, try walking into a store in the mall. Just about all of the time the sales person will walk right up to you and ask if you need any help. Most of the time, however, you will respond with a no. At that point the sales person will either walk away or make it a point to say that everything in the store is twenty percent off. The reason you say you don't need any help is because you don't feel comfortable with this person yet. If the salesman were to start building a rapport with the customer, you would see the customer become much more receptive to what they have to offer.

What you will learn in this book is how to be the complete opposite of most salespeople. When we think about being too much about the sale we think of car salesmen. You know, that awful feeling when you walk into a car dealership. Ultimately, what most people do not want is to be pressured into buying a product or service. The question really is, then why do we do exactly that? Spending most of your time, not trying to sell your product, but rather understanding the needs and wants of the customer is far more powerful. You will also learn how to be more comfortable if someone objects to a sale. Learning the four steps to overcoming objections will help you in any sales situation. The biggest problem most people make when someone objects is that they lack empathy toward the customer. Without empathy, most people will fail in trying to overcome a customer's objection. One needs to really understand why someone said no before they come up with a potential solution

I started my career selling fitness. Fitness comes in various forms whether it is a gym membership or personal training package. It is very hard for a personal trainer in their young twenty's to ask a customer to spend a thousand dollars for a fitness package. I then thought that by giving a customer a great workout, the customer would then buy a fitness package. Over time I realized that it is never about what you are selling. In fact, if you think your product is great you are missing the point on how to be great at sales. I like to call this phenomenon *"The Starbucks Effect"* which we will go into detail later on in this book. Like the C.E.O. of Starbucks, Howard Schultz, say's-it's not about the coffee. I learned that the more I focused on building a great connection, the more customers were willing to give me a shot as a trainer. As my business grew, so did my understanding of the sales process. The biggest takeaway was that although I considered myself a great trainer, I needed to become great at building relationships first. Selling someone on the idea of what they could become was more powerful than me discounting a personal training package. Having always been in the top five percent in revenue of any company I have worked for, I put the pen to paper to help others at this process.

CHAPTER 1

People Don't Buy Products Until They Believe In Them

I BELIEVE THAT most salespeople suck at sales. Ok, I agree maybe the word "suck" is too harsh so let's say you're just "average" at sales. Either way it's not what you should be striving for in business. In order to not "suck", one needs to understand what "not" to do. People ask me all the time to teach them sales. My reply is always that sales are just transactions. Taking my credit card and running a payment is a sale. What I can teach people is the philosophy that goes into that transaction. In life we are constantly confronted with sales people. Whether it is advertisements in the mail, the early evening knock at the door from your rival cable company trying to get you to switch over or the late night cold call to your home phone trying to get you to buy All Sate Insurance instead of State Farm. Now I will say, if you happen to still have a landline then you deserve that call. In reality, life is sales. We are always selling whether you know it or not. Have you ever tried to get your friend to try a restaurant that you love or getting someone to watch your favorite television show? You are "selling" them on an idea.

My favorite movie clip comes from the classic "The Wolf of Wall Street" starring Leonardo DiCaprio. Leo plays the infamous Jordan Belfort who made millions selling stocks. In 1999, Jordan pleaded guilty to fraud and other crimes in connection with stock-market manipulation and running a boiler room as part of a penny-stock scam (Wikipedia). That, however, is not the point of this story. During the movie, Leonardo DiCaprio is trying to teach his misfit friends into becoming great junk bond salesman. In one of the most iconic scenes, Leo is discussing the art of sales, so he turns to his friend and say's:

"Sell me this pen"

What makes most people average at sales is they find themselves talking about the product. I mean to the average person that makes sense right? After all you're trying to sell someone a pen, so how can you not talk about it. When presented with this challenge the friend starts to fumble his way through a sales pitch:

"This is the best pen ever made", he says.

"This may be the last pen you ever buy"

One by one his friends fall by the waste side in trying to sell Leo the pen. The fact of the matter, however, is that it is not about the pen but rather what the result will yield. You see it's never about the product. In fact, a pen is just a pen so if you are selling me on the idea of that, I'm really not interested. Getting back to the movie, the friends struggle with coming up with words to try and sell the pen. At this point in the scene another friend grabs the pen, slides a piece of paper in front of Leo and say's:

"Do me a favor and sign this piece of paper"

Leo says:

"Well I don't have a pen"

The friend says:

"Oh, you don't have a pen anymore. Supply and demand, bro."

You see it's about what a product can do for you. In this case the ability to sign your name. No one buys a car but rather the ability to drive. No one buys a gym membership but rather the ability to achieve their fitness goal and no one purchases clothing but rather the ability to be seen in a fashionable light. Stop selling pens and start selling ideas. People don't buy until they believe.

Almost every top company in the world has a belief system in which it communicates to you, the consumer, via their marketing message. The message that such companies convey to the consumer, I believe, is what makes a company either great or just like everyone else. If you are in sales your goal should always be to strive to be number one. No one remembers who came in second. Usane Bolt won the one hundred meter dash in the Rio Olympics. Does anybody remember who came in second? One of my favorite philosophies in business comes from Simon Sinek's "The Golden Circle" (See figure 1):

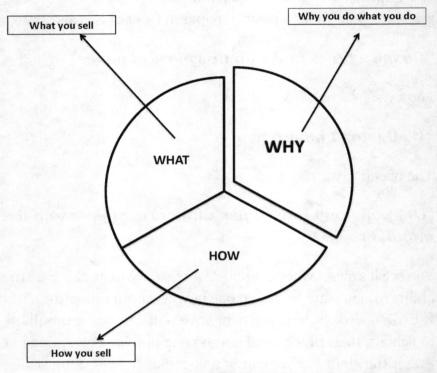

(Figure 1:The Golden Circle-Simon Sinek)

You see The Golden Circle teaches us three simple words in business- "What", "How" and "Why". Although all of them are important to answer in business, only the best companies focus more on the "Why". For this example let us take a look at one of the top companies in the world-Apple. Most people in today's society not only have an Apple product but most have more than one (i.e. phone and laptop). When I am teaching sales to the fitness industry, I always make it a point to ask how many people have at least one Apple product. Usually about eighty percent of every class I teach has at least one. Here is what I find interesting about Apple and its competitors. Let us take a look at Apple's competition in the industry (see figure 2):

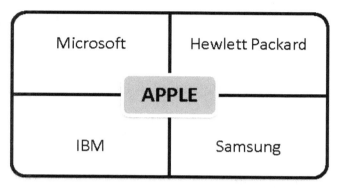

(Figure 2: APPLE competition)

APPLE COMPETITORS MARKET VALUE
(Statista 2017):

1. Microsoft- $507 billion
2. Samsung- $254 billion
3. IBM- $162 billion
4. Hewlett Packard- $29 billion

APPLE MARKET VALUE- $752 billion

To put it into perspective, in 2015, Apple had a ninety-four percent share of the world's global smartphone profits and sold the only profitable smart watch and tablets *(Source:*

Appleinsider.com). I once read that one of Apple's keys when designing a product is that it must be something that the designer would want him/herself. Meaning, these represent real customers.

What I find interesting is that if you take a look at the following three aspects of the business, each of Apple's competitors can match Apple in that area and yet Apple remains far and above the rest in branding and profit.

1. STAFFING

All of Apple's competitors have the same access that Apple has when it comes to hiring the right people and staffing. Whether they pluck them from Silicon Valley or scour all of the technology Universities, they all have the same access to the same talent. Not only can the other companies hire the same people but they can also pay them more than Apple if they choose.

2. TECHNOLOGY

All of these companies have access to all of the same technology. If you really look at what a Samsung phone, for example, can do versus an Apple phone it is relatively the same. There is not much that Apple can do that is widely different than all of the competition in the field of technology. In fact, some studies show that Samsung is actually a better phone than Apple's IPhone.

3. MARKETING DOLLARS

This, to me, is the most interesting one of the three. Yes, all of Apple's competition can pour the same amount of dollars into marketing that Apple could. Whether it is commercials, social media or spokespeople, they all can do the same thing. It is in this category, however, where I think Apple separates themselves from the rest.

So why is Apple the number one company in the world when all of the other companies can do what Apple does? Once I understood that focusing on a companies belief system or philosophy is more powerful than the "what" or "how" a company works, it made perfect sense. You see most companies spend most of their time and money talking about "What" and "How" they do things and that is how they communicate their message to you the consumer. I bet you have never heard an Apple commercial that focused on a sale or promotion that they may be having? In fact, the IPhone X retails for one thousand dollars, which by the way sold out within an hour of its release. It always comes back to how much value you place on a product or service rather than the price itself. Does price factor in? Absolutely but it is not the deciding factor.

You see Apple spends their dollars talking about their philosophy. I mean everyone already knows "What" and "How" Apple does things. This is the message you really hear from Apple in any marketing commercial:

"We believe we can change the way people communicate around the world. Do you want to be part of our community?"

The answer is simply…yes! The message that Apple communicates is all about community and family. In fact, have you ever walked into a Microsoft store in the mall? It is one of the best-designed stores that I have ever seen. The inside of the retail store is modern looking and sleek. One entire wall, in fact, is an X-Box screen that you can play video games on. Picture playing a video game where the screen is an entire wall. Conversely, have you ever walked into an Apple store? It is just wooden tables with its product on it and yet Apple consistently dominates the market. Can you imagine, back in the day, when Apple was going over the design for their first ever retail store? I imagine Apple employees coming up with the most mind blowing retail store. I am sure senior executives wanted to make it really futuristic and edgy looking. At some point, however, someone must have stood up in the meeting and said:

"Let's just have tables with the product on it."

And then they actually went with that idea. That is why Steve Jobs was a genius.

Apple understands that it is not about the product or their store design but rather the unique ability to get people to believe in what they sell. Only the best companies in the world share this one philosophy. They all have that common theme of speaking to the customer's emotions and why you should buy their product.

I thought it would be a great idea to look at some of the top Chief Executive Officers and their philosophies on how they run/ran their companies:

WAL-MART:

"Leadership through service" was Sam Walton's vision when creating Wal-Mart. He believed that true leadership depends on willing service and so it became the founding principle on which the company started from. In 1962 Sam Walton opened the first Wal-Mart with the premise built on the idea of offering lower prices with great service. This was a principle Sam's competitors thought was crazy. This, however, was the reason that in 1970 the company went public. His profits even exceeded Sam's expectations. He credited the rapid growth to not just the lower prices but also the great associates that worked at Wal-Mart who offered a great shopping experience.

> "
>
> *The secret of successful retailing is to give people what they want. And really if you think about it from the point of view of the customer, you want everything: a wide assortment of good quality merchandise; the lowest possible prices; guaranteed satisfaction; pleasant shopping experience"*
> ...Sam Walton
>
> "

Having been a frequent shopper at Wal-Mart, I believe that they have the two most important ingredients for a successful business- low pricing and great customer service.

VIRGIN AMERICA:

Whenever you talk about Sir Richard Branson, Chief Executive Officer of Virgin, you talk about the art of mastering customer service. He very often talks about his seven rules to success. Rule number two is my favorite.

RULE 2: Express a passionate commitment to serving the customer.

Ok so that's all well and good, I mean what company doesn't want that. Let's take a look at how that really works. If you talk to most companies and ask, "what business are you in" they would simply say the business of whatever product that they sell. For example, most airlines Chief Executive Officers when asked, "what business are you in" would reply with probably one answer, "the airline business". When that question was posed to Sir Richard Branson he replied *"the experience business"*. Quite a departure from most and the point is just that. Stop being like everyone else and start thinking about the consumer and the experience they deserve. If you think about the airline business, all the major airlines buy planes from the same manufacturers (Boeing or Airbus) so then what makes Virgin, Virgin? I had the privilege to experience a Virgin flight and it was just that... an experience. As soon as you get on the flight you notice the fluorescent pink lighting illuminating the cabin. I felt like I was at a club in the Hamptons rather than a metal tube about to defy gravity. I sat down and noticed the television monitors had remote controls where not only can you text message friends and family but you can order drinks to your seat as well. Finally, the flight attendants break out into song describing how the seat can be used as a flotation device. I felt like I was at a showing of Hamilton but it was just the flight attendants way of going over the safety precautions. So yes they are different and yes it is an experience. Can you really say that every airline does it this way?

> "
>
> **"When we started Virgin Atlantic thirty years ago we had one 747 and we were competing with airlines that had an avg. of 300 planes each. Every single one of those airlines has gone bankrupt because they didn't have customer service. In the end its all about customer service"**
> .... Sir Richard Branson
>
> "

DISNEY:

The fact is, is that Disney is the Gold standard for almost every company when it comes to customer experience. It is like they say, **"it's the happiest place on earth"**, I mean where else can a two-year old have just as much fun as a fifty-year old. Disney's philosophy is called "Guest-ology" and deals with four directions of their business- Needs, Wants, Stereotypes and Emotions.

NEEDS: When Disney talks about the needs it's always about meeting the requirements of the guest. That means at the very least a family visiting Disney needs a pass to get in, food to eat and attractions to experience. Meeting at least the minimum requirements of every guest is essential.

WANTS: When Disney talks about wants its code for going the extra mile. Sure they need rides to ride but some want to skip the line so they don't have to wait. Fast-pass allows for that very want to happen. When you combine the minimum requirements and then add in specific wants, you start to create more than just an average experience.

STEREOTYPES: Everyone has a pre-conceived notion before you go somewhere and it's where you start to form positive and negative thoughts. Most people probably feel that they will have to wait in massive lines at Disney and start to form a negative impression. Not only does Disney have the Fast-Pass discussed earlier but they also use technology to their advantage. When you go to Disney you get a "Magic Band" and mobile app., which allows you to see the wait times of any ride wherever you are at in the park. Overcoming the stereotype is key in their equation.

EMOTIONS: Emotions are by far the most important. Tap into that and you have created a great experience for the guest. If you don't believe me, have your son or daughter meet Mickey Mouse for the first time and then you will know what I'm talking about. I recently visited Disney with my two-year old son, Kameron. I purchased a special ticket for one hundred dollars where at eight p.m. I can meet Mickey Mouse privately and take some pictures. For one-hour I was cursing under my breathe as I waited on this never ending line. That was, of course, until my son came face to face with "Mr. Mouse" himself. The look on his face made that one-hour, one hundred dollar fee completely disappear.

A sale is all about making an emotional connection.

> *"You don't build it for yourself.*
> *You know what people want and*
> *you build it for them"*
> ...Walt Disney

All of these top visionaries had one common theme...it's all about the consumer. Much of my own success in sales comes from the idea that in order to sell, one must not. In other words don't sell a product but rather build value in that product. The best way to do this is to build rapport with the customer. I mean genuine rapport and not the fake kind. For example, many people say to start out with a compliment. That only works if it's genuine. If you just compliment someone and then move right on to what your selling then it really doesn't get you anywhere.

"How are you doing this morning? By the way I like your shirt. Hey are you interested in what I have to sell?"

If your going to compliment someone on their shirt then you should actually have a little bit more of a conversation around the shirt...where did you buy it from or how much did you pay for it? Remember people don't buy products until they believe in them. Meaning if someone doesn't believe in the product or service then the chances of you making a sale is really slim. Building genuine trust with that guest makes it

14

easier to believe in what you are selling. If you look at some of the companies mentioned previously, they didn't build their belief system around pricing but rather a belief system that revolves around customer experience. It's one hundred and fifty dollars for a day pass at Disney World. Do you think the employees who work the ticket counter are afraid to tell you the price of the ticket? It is simply that every tourist that plans on going to Disney believes in what Disney offers and the experience it yields. No one has ever said to me you have to fly Virgin America because the prices are the cheapest. Consumers fly Virgin because they know or heard that the experience you get is second to none. Finally an IPhone is eight hundred and fifty dollars retail but you would be pressed to find a "genius" in an Apple store that is afraid to tell you the price.

QUESTION:

#1 reason why salespeople do not make a sale?

ANSWER:

They don't ask for it

You did not read that wrong, most sales people actually get so nervous that they forget to actually ask for the sale. So many times, however, I see sales people dance around the price in their presentation. You see this in all industries. In my industry, the fitness industry, you see both sales advisors and personal trainers hit this roadblock frequently. A sales advisor gives an awesome tour of their health club and then you can see he/she starts to become nervous, as they get closer to talking about pricing. People don't buy until they believe. You

15

see if you truly believe in what you are selling then the price is worth it. More importantly if you can build a relationship around the product your chances of selling that product increase exponentially.

A personal trainer actually has a tougher job than the sales advisor. At this point a person has already spent their dollars on a gym membership so a personal trainer has to get that person to spend additional money on their services. Once again a trainer gives a member a fantastic complimentary session, as most gyms do, and then their teeth start to chatter as they ask the person if they want to spend eight hundred dollars on a fitness package. When I first started out in the business I was terrified to ask for money. As I look back on those days it was the most nerve racking part of an assessment. Eight hundred dollars is a lot of money to me and that, ironically, is the problem with most sales people. What you perceive as a lot does not mean the person you are trying to sell your product to does. Stop thinking with your own wallet and start building value in what you sell.

Think about the average person who has tried to lose thirty pounds his/her entire life. The yoyo dieting here and there yields some success at different periods of time in their life but never sustainable. They then meet a fitness professional who, not only, is able to build value in why that person should be working with a trainer but actually is able to help that person lose thirty pounds. So the question becomes is eight hundred dollars worth that? You bet it is and even though it is a lot of money it is totally worth it in the end.

When I used to sell personal training I wasn't confident in the product that I was selling. More importantly I never gave a reason why someone should work with me. I mean I thought I did because I said things like

"I am the best trainer"

or

"I always get results"

When I thought about the fact that people don't buy products, they need to believe in them first is when I realized how I should be communicating to people. I started communicating this message:

"What I am going to do with you is hold you accountable to a healthier lifestyle. We are going to accomplish this together by focusing on not just our workouts in the gym but everything you do outside the gym"

This is how I got people to believe in what I was selling. Remember that everyone knows what a personal trainer sells-*training*. Everyone also knows how a trainer might get you to buy training-*free session*. The differentiator is when you talk about "Why" someone would want to buy training from you. It is the fact that we are going to work together as a team, as well as, having accountability during the process. That is how you reach your goals.

> ❝
> *"People don't buy what you do,*
> *they buy why you do it"*
> - Simon Sinek
> ❞

CHAPTER 2
The Big Three

EVERY TIME I finish a speaking engagement for sales I always ask the audience if they have any questions. I find it interesting, however, that most people do not take the time to really understand some key sales statistics. At the end of the day, a sale is a transaction that is based in philosophy. The following facts are some of my favorite ones about sales as an industry. They, more or less, can relate to any business, which makes it that more imperative that you take the time to understand and learn each one. Each statistic has its source labeled. In no particular order:

1. 92% OF ALL CUSTOMER INTERACTIONS HAPPEN OVER THE PHONE.
(Source: Brian Williams, Brevit Group.)

One of the most common questions people ask me is how to make phone calls. Yes it sounds dumb but phone calls actually require skill and a level of strategy. The reason people struggle with this skill is because they are afraid or nervous of one simple word-REJECTION. It is not in our nature to accept rejection but it is part of any sales game. Phone calls will result in many "no's". You need to first accept and embrace that fact. Building rapport on the phone can be done but it requires the sales person to ask open-ended questions. Digging deep and trying to figure out why a person might want your product or service is far more important than just giving your product out. Open-ended questions will allow a person to have more of a conversation rather than just answering with a yes or no.

2. IT TAKES AN AVERAGE OF 8 COLD CALL ATTEMPTS TO REACH A PROSPECT.

(Source: Brian Williams, Brevit Group.)

Yes, eight attempts which is why most people fail at calls. They usually give up or they feel that they are bothering a person if they call. Think about calling someone eight times and how easy it is to give up after just calling them twice. That, however, is what separates the great sales people from everyone else. Make sure to mark down on your calendar the day and time you make each call so you can reference that each time you call back. As a general rule, one call every three days is a good starting point. A best practice should also be to leave a voice message stating that you look forward to speaking and that you will call back in a few days. This lets the person know that you will be trying again to get a hold of him or her.

3. THE BEST TIME TO COLD CALL IS BE-TWEEN 4:00 AND 5:00 PM.

(Source: Brian Williams, Brevit Group.)

Don't be so shocked. Many employees that I know make their calls in the morning. If you think about when someone is the most rushed or have the most on their mind it usually is in the morning. Whether it's getting the kids ready for school or putting the finishing touches on a presentation you are doing in front of the board that day. That being said time and time again I hear employees call their leads first thing in the morning. Do you want to pick up a sales call at eight in the morning? This certainly doesn't mean you can't call in the morning but understand it is not the best time to call. It also depends upon your schedule and if you only work in the mornings or not. If you do, you might want to take the call list home with you and try different times.

4. 80% OF SALES REQUIRE 5 FOLLOW-UP CALLS AFTER THE INITIAL MEETING. 44% OF SALES REPS GIVE UP AFTER 1 FOLLOW-UP.

(Source: Brian Williams, Brevit Group.)

Need I say more? One of the key factors in sales is to stay persistent. I mean almost half lose out to a sale because they didn't simply attempt a few more calls. Coming from the health and fitness industry I see this quite a bit. A potential member comes in to see if they like the gym or not but decide that they are just shopping around. The sales advisor then calls back one time, a day later and then gives up on that person. They tend to forget about the lead because they feel as if they weren't going to buy anything in the first place. Judging people on their actions is a big mistake in sales. Just because a person does not call you back after two attempts does not mean that they are not interested in what you are selling. Stay persistent and consistent when making calls because it can really pay off in the end.

5. THURSDAY IS THE BEST DAY TO PROSPECT. WEDNESDAY IS THE SECOND BEST DAY.
(Source: Brian Williams, Brevit Group.)

Now, of course this doesn't mean you can't on any other day but it does mean that in sales there is a strategy. Think about someone's mindset on Thursday rather than Monday. It's almost the weekend as opposed to just starting out the week. When a sales person starts thinking about the guests needs, wants and mindset and stops putting his/her needs first then that's when the sales person will make a personal connection.

6. 78% OF SALESPEOPLE USING SOCIAL MEDIA OUTSELL THEIR PEERS.
(Source: Brian Williams, Brevit Group.)

I know everyone was waiting to hear those two words- Social Media. Social Media is part of our fabric and even dominating sales in certain instances. Always make sure whatever social media you are leveraging that it is professional to the eye. Effective social media campaigns can be so effective as long as it is consistent. Does Apple just make one advertisement and then only post it once? Advertising through social media should be a constant effort with only the actual messaging changing from time to time.

7. EMAIL IS ALMOST 40 TIMES BETTER AT ACQUIRING NEW CUSTOMERS THAN FACEBOOK AND TWITTER.

(Source: Brian Williams, Brevit Group.)

Now that you're bought into social media lets not forget that it is still more effective to email someone when given the chance. It is a lot more personal and at the end of the day the more you can build rapport on a personal level the better chances you have to make a sales connection with the person. Emails effectively break down the sales wall that every person has when confronted with a sales pitch. With an email you can sit and read it in the comfort of your own home with no added sales pressure. I used to work at a big time gym chain in New York. The first task I did when I arrived was to send an email to existing members, asking them if they received their free personal training session that came with their gym membership. In the email I made it a point to really go over what to expect during the one-hour session. What this did is really convey to the member how important it was to come to that session. The end result was that I was able to get in about forty percent of the members for that free session. I credit a really effective email for that.

8. SALESPEOPLE WHO ACTIVELY SEEK OUT AND EXPLOIT REFERRALS EARN 4 TO 5 TIMES MORE THAN THOSE WHO DON'T.

(Source: Brian Williams, Brevit Group.)

Here is a stat for you. The number one reason a person doesn't get a referral is because they don't ask. Some people get so excited after making a sale that they actually forget to ask for a referral. That's right it sounds baffling but it's the truth. Think about how hard you work on one particular individual trying to make a sale. Then after all of that time you actually make the sale. I don't blame you for being really excited and relieved but that's also the reason you forget to ask for a referral. Put a post-it note somewhere on your desk to actually remind you to ask for a referral. It actually will help. Another great tip when it comes to getting referrals is to assume that you will get them. A big mistake sales people make is to say things like "do you have any friends or family?" rather than "think of one person who you want to come in and experience what you did. Who is it and when can I call them to introduce myself?" Assume you will get a referral and that the only thing you need to do to get it is ask.

9. ONLY 13% OF CUSTOMERS BELIEVE A SALES PERSON CAN UNDERSTAND THEIR NEEDS.
(Source: Brian Williams, Brevit Group.)

Frankly it is why I'm writing this book. You need to build rapport and understand what the customer wants in order to make a sale. Sales based on building relationships are how to be really effective. In fact what your going to learn in the next few chapters is how NOT to sell. Don't worry it will all make sense soon. Building value versus just throwing your product in someone's face as soon as you meet him or her is far more effective in making a sale. Most people in sales get nervous about making the sale, which means they truly do not stop to really listen to a customer and what he/she really is looking for. Active listening plays a huge role on building a successful relationship in sales. We all know how it feels when you're talking to someone and they aren't really paying attention to what you are saying. Active listening means to stop being in such a hurry to talk. In sales we think that we need to get out all of the information about what we are selling but if you let the customer tell you what they really want, you wont need to talk as much.

10. 55% OF THE PEOPLE MAKING THEIR LIVING IN SALES DON'T HAVE THE RIGHT SKILLS TO BE SUCCESSFUL.
(Source: Brian Williams, Brevit Group.)

Need I say more? The more proactive you are, the more you will further educate yourself on sales. Whether it is books or seminars there are plenty of learning tools out in the world now. You just have to want it bad enough. One of the ways I used to educate myself on sales is looking at some You Tube videos, books and attending some seminars. Since I traveled a lot, I would plug in my headphones and listen to some of the top people in the business (i.e. John C. Maxwell, Simon Sinek). This is how I learned some of the techniques I still use today and how I formulated my own theories and processes for selling. Every good sales person has the ability to learn information but then create a personal story behind it. This is important because it should be and sound genuine. Give consumers credit; if **you** don't believe in what you selling **they** will know it.

11. RESEARCH SHOWS THAT 30%-50%OF SALES GOES TO THE VENDOR THAT RE-SPONDS FIRST.

(Source: insidesales.com)

This basically tells you that when you get a lead, you better call them within the first twenty-four hours. So many times sales people have a call list, that sometimes, goes untouched for days until the sales person gets around to calling. If you are competing against other companies, which most of the time you are, get on that phone and call right away. You never know who else might be beating you to the punch. Having a standard time of the day that is set aside for calls will also help you stay consistent. Once you get into a routine you will be able to stay up to date with your call log. Always remember that if your not calling, someone else is.

12. ONLY 25% OF LEADS ARE LEGITIMATE AND SHOULD ADVANCE TO SALES.

(Source: Gleanster Research)

One simple phrase when it comes to sales-it's a numbers game. In my early sales career, I remember being so excited to get a lead. Some days I would get more than one and as my career grew so did my number of leads per day. What I soon learned, however, was that getting a lead was only half the battle. The other half was getting them to come in. So think about this statistic as you move forward in your career. If you were to go out and get one hundred leads today, only twenty-five would advance to a sale. More important than getting the lead is also making sure that they set an appointment. The only reason that someone sets up an appointment is if they view it as having some value or benefit to him or herself. When calling prospects, make it a point to really connect with someone on the phone. It is not just about what you are selling. We talked earlier that open-ended questions with a customer is a great way to build rapport.

13. 70% OF PEOPLE MAKE PURCHASING DECISIONS TO SOLVE PROBLEMS. 30% MAKE DECISIONS TO GAIN SOMETHING

(Source: Impact Communications)

One of my favorite lines to remember in sales is to- Be The Solution. If seventy percent of people making purchases need to solve a problem then find the solution. Very often we want to sell a product or idea and yet we will not take the time to understand if the potential buyer actually can benefit from it. The fitness industry is a great example of this. Every sales advisor at every gym has one mission, which is to sell gym memberships. Most of the time, however, they do not really take the time to understand why a customer would want to join in the first place. Are there really meaningful conversations wrapped around the customers fitness goals, probably not. What the sales advisor typically does is give a generic tour and then lays the price onto the customer. I always tell people that there is only one reason why a person would use a guest pass at a gym, join that gym and then even buy training from a trainer. The answer is to reach their fitness goals and yet the person's fitness goals are barely mentioned on a sales call. What makes a great call effective is making sure you have some relative notes on that person. In this case what the person's fitness goals are. Most sales people think that the purpose of a phone call is to get the customer to buy something or set up an appointment. The real purpose of a call is to find out what the customer's needs are and then the result of the phone call should be to set up an appointment. Let me say that one more time because I find this to always be a sticking point with people in sales. The actual purpose of making a call or connecting with a customer is to specifically find out what he/she is looking for. The result of this process is the appointment or sale.

14. PERSONLIZED EMAILS INCLUDING THE RECIPIENT'S FIRST NAME IN THE SUBJECT LINE HAVE HIGHER OPEN RATES.

(Source: Retention Science)

I once worked for a popular gym chain in NY City as a Fitness Manager. When I first arrived I wanted to email all of the new members and introduce myself to them. After gathering the enormous list of existing members I proceeded to write them all an introduction email. I remember, however, that in every subject line I wrote:

Att: Name

What I was doing was personalizing every email. How many

emails do you not open just based on the subject line alone. Sounds miniscule but I bet you it is a lot. Thirty to forty percent of all emails I had sent putting the customer's names in the subject line were responded to. A sale is all about building rapport, even through emails.

15. 83% OF CUSTOMERS ARE COMFORTABLE MAKING A REFERRAL AFTER A POSTIVE EXPERIENCE.
(Source: Texas Tech University)

You will always hear me say that what makes a sale is a great experience. The power of that cannot only have a great effect with that person but with their friends and family as well. Eight out of ten people will give you a referral if they received a great experience. That shows how powerful building rapport can really be. The number one reason, as discussed earlier, a salesperson does not make a sale is because they don't ask. Similarly, the number one reason why a sales person doesn't get a referral is that they don't ask.

Now that you understand a little bit more about trends in sales, let us take a look at what has helped me in the past and how I use philosophy in sales to my advantage.

THE BIG 3

What I have learned in the past twenty years is that you can study everything about a subject and look at every statistic but that alone doesn't guarantee success. There are many factors that go into becoming great at sales. One of the biggest mistakes I see in sales is the lack of what I like to call "The Big 3" (see figure 3). "The Big 3" are the aspects of learning that, when put together, can truly help you become great at your craft. Now most people in sales practice one or two of these learning techniques but not all three. When you both stay consistent, as well as, persistent with these three techniques, you will understand that sales are much more than having a sale or promotion for what you are selling.

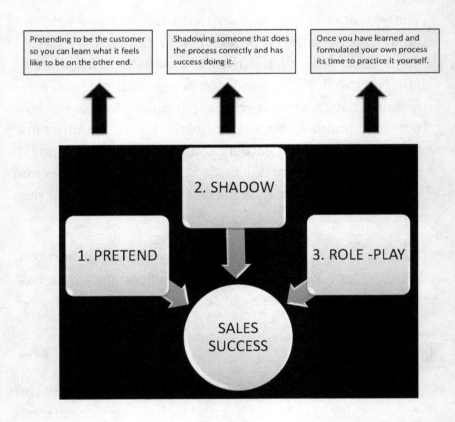

(Figure 3:The Big 3)

1. PRETEND:

When I first started out as a young sales person in the fitness industry I found myself having trouble selling. Specifically my job was to sell personal training packages. I used to think that if you offer someone a special rate or tell him or her that we are having a sale today, it would intrigue the buyer even more. That, however, wasn't the case most of the time. I decided to walk into my local car dealer to "pretend" to lease a car. So the question is, what does pretending to lease a car have anything to do with selling fitness? The answer; EVERYTHING! You see what I learned was what not to do. Anybody who has ever walked into a car dealership knows exactly what I am talking about. You sit down with the dealer after looking at what model car your interested in and then "it" happens. "It" is the typical sales experience. The salesman offers you the price at which point you politely say:

"That is more than I would like to pay per month"

So the car dealer excuses him or herself only to come back with a different price. Now at this point although the price has magically decreased it is still not in the ballpark of reality and in accordance with your finances. So the car dealer excuses him or herself again and comes over with, you guessed it, the manager. You know when the manager comes over its time to negotiate. The problem I have with this is that at no point did the car dealer ask my permission to bring over the manager. It would have been different if he had said:

"Do you mind if I introduce you to the manager. Maybe he can come up with a better price?"

At which point I would have said:

"Definitely"

Pretending is a great way to see what not or what to do in certain areas of sales. I then progressed from car dealers to walking into gyms to pretend to buy a membership. What I got from this was invaluable since this was my professional field. I would learn what a "museum tour" was where the sales person just shows you everything the gym has to offer. I learned how sales people tried to build rapport by starting with a compliment and if it was a real or fake one. Never take for granted how much you can learn from walking into an establishment and pretending to buy something. This process allows you to look at things from a customer's point of view. One-mistake sales people make is they try and sell what "they" think you want versus what "you" really want. It is a fundamental flaw in sales. We do this because we fail to put ourselves in the customer's shoes. One of the biggest lessons I learned was that to truly build rapport and a great experience you really need to understand the needs and wants of the customer.

2. SHADOWING:

One of the most forgotten arts in sales has to be shadowing. One of the reasons why I was so successful at different points in my life at sales was because I learned from the best. The way I learned was through shadowing. If there was a trainer who was great at selling training packages I would make it a point to ask if I can shadow him or her the next time they have an assessment. Now in today's world, many good managers build shadowing into their on-boarding process. This is really effective in gathering the tools to go into your tool belt of sales. I learned a little bit from each person I shadowed until I was able to formulate my own process to sell. Here is the critical component of shadowing. You must get great coaching from the people that you are shadowing. Spending time watching them is not enough. You need to have conversations with mentors to find out how they think in certain situations. When you partner shadowing of great people with great coaching, you have the recipe for great success in sales. It is really important to see someone do a sales process both correctly and successfully. This will help to download information into the brain as to what "good" looks like.

3. ROLE -PLAY:

If Michael Jordan or LeBron James has to practice then so do you. It amazes me how ill prepared people are at their jobs. Anyone attending one of my sales classes knows that they will be role-playing in front of the class. It is one of my favorite aspects of teaching. If you really want to see someone perform under pressure then sit him or her down in front of a class and tell them to role-play. Chances are that no one usually nails it the first or even second time. In fact, my feeling on role-paly is that it is more for the people watching. Very often the longer you watch someone role-play the better you are at it when it is your turn. There is not that rush of adrenaline when you are just watching so you are able to take in the information a lot better. It also reinforces what you just learned and allows you to actually practice it with real human interaction. It doesn't take long for the human brain to remember what it needs to say. This skill, however, doesn't remain unless you have constant practice. One of the tricks I used to do when it comes to role-play was to pull out my IPhone recorder and tape myself. There is nothing worse than listening to you try and sell something. Although hard to listen to it does make you better at selling. Since role-playing is part of how I teach it is fascinating how people have different learning curves. Even when you feel comfortable with your material it is still important to keep those skills sharp. Sales is also cyclical in that you will have days, weeks or months when you have little success and then other times when your "killing" it. That is why it is so important to never lose sight of how powerful practice and role-play could be.

"

"People don't ask for facts in making up their minds. They would rather have one good, soul-satisfying emotion than a dozen facts."
– Robert Keith Leavit

"

CHAPTER 3

Value Proposition

The Starbucks Effect

LET ME START out by saying that Starbucks to me is average tasting coffee. That being said, every day, twice a day, no matter what state I am in I buy a Grande Pike from Starbucks for two dollars and forty cents. If the coffee is average tasting to me then WHY do I buy it twice a day? I mean there are plenty of other places I can, not only buy better tasting coffee, but for much cheaper as well. Yet, everyday, twice a day, I seek out a Starbucks. Thank God for Google maps when I travel because all I have to do is type in Starbucks and my phone does the rest. To answer WHY I do this everyday, twice a day, you need to understand what value proposition is. So let us take a look at why value proposition is so important in sales.

Definition: **Value Proposition-**

A belief from the customer about how value will be delivered experienced and acquired. A value proposition can apply to an entire organization, or parts thereof, or customer accounts, or products or services. Creating a value proposition is part of a business strategy. (Source: Wikipedia)

So what does that mean? Well let's put you in Vegas. Whether you have never been there before and it's your first time or you're a seasoned veteran, you are there now. Now let's take something that you buy everyday. For me, it is coffee but maybe it is a Monster drink, Red Bull or just a bottle of water. Let's use a two dollar and forty cents amount as an example, which will represent that product that you buy everyday. You traditionally spend a certain amount of money on that product that you have everyday so I want you to remember that amount as we move forward in this example. Now let's say two days have passed because of the long flight and your robust Vegas schedule of going out and partying each night. So two days have passed and you have NOT had that very thing that you tend to have every single day. Here's the best part, you are sitting by the pool in Vegas and you see what looks like a waitress holding a tray. Now that's not the best part, but on the tray is that very product that you buy everyday. At first you think it is just a mirage but it's actually that two dollar and forty cents product. The waitress then approaches and says:

"Would you like to purchase one"?

Without hesitation you say:

"Of course"

At which point the waitress says:

"It will be two dollars and seventy five cents"

Now I will bet that at least nine out of ten of people would not hesitate to purchase the product. Not only that but we can play this game until we get to a point that you are not willing to spend any more money. Most people would probably pay more than three dollars for that product given the situation. So the question is, how did I effectively get you to spend more money than you normally do each and every day for that product? The reason is because you value that product because you know the result it has on you. That is VALUE PROPOSITION. I value Starbucks because of the EXPERIENCE I get when I go there. Build a great experience and I promise that you will create value. When I talk about the Starbucks effect, I want you to think about what experience I am truly getting. Before I tell you about that experience and how that alone gets me to walk into a Starbucks, I want to talk about the opposite effect first. Let us first talk about how a poor experience can lose a sale.

There is no better example than what I like to call "The most dreaded kiosk in every mall". You know those kiosks in the middle of every mall in America. I have been telling this story for two years and honestly, it never gets old. The reason why it never gets old is because when I tell you that I love to teach how not to sell, this example is the complete opposite. In fact, if you really want to learn how NOT to be effective at sales one needs to look no further than this kiosk. So which one am I talking about- cell phones, hair extensions, as seen on TV? This example is all about "sea salt lotion from the Dead Sea". Now, do not act like you do not know what I'm talking about. It's the one where they try and get you to wash your hands in their nice, porcelain bowl at which point they try to scrub and exfoliate your arms with sea salt lotion from the Dead Sea. Usually it's two beautiful women working the kiosk and I would be remised if I didn't say that I was suckered one time into seeing what it was all about. What makes this the most dreaded kiosk in America is that they basically drag you over. You can be walking right near their lotion stand and boom; they jump right in front of you. Talk about being in your personal space.

This story happened a few years ago one-week prior to Thanksgiving. I had traveled to Florida to teach a group of sales advisors for the first time at a gym chain I was working for. The course is two-days and very often after day one I have the entire afternoon free. When I have afternoons off, I love to go shopping. There are two reasons I love to shop:

Reason #1: I love to sub-consciously evaluate sales people when I walk into stores (I can't help it).

Reason #2: I just love to buy things.

So after day one of teaching I asked some of the locals where the nearest mall was. They said it was only a few miles away so, of course, I was pumped. I get to the mall and as I walk through it, I saw that infamous kiosk. Now, normally I would do what any rational guy in this situation would do and that is to pull out my phone and pretend to talk to someone as I walk by. Having a fake conversation assures me, of course, of not having to deal with the two "Master" salesmen of lotion. Not only would I have a fake conversation on my phone but I would walk as far away from the kiosk as possible. The last thing anyone wants to do is to make eye contact.

This particular day, however, was different. What was different this time was that there were two men working the kiosk, which I have never seen before. What I noticed, however, was that the one gentleman was walking right in front of people to try and get them to walk over to the kiosk. Here were my two thoughts, which at the time seemed great.

1. That guy had great energy because he was walking toward everyone
2. He wasn't afraid to talk to anyone.

Now, at the time I thought given these two characteristics, what a great candidate to be a sales advisor at our gym in Florida. I mean having great energy and the ability to talk to everyone is the Gold standard in the fitness industry. So, instead of having a fake conversation on my phone I decided to approach the guy and introduce myself. Once again, seemed like a great idea at the time. I made a bee line for the guy, walked up and said:

"Hi, my name is Kory and I work for ____gym. I have to say I love your energy. Have you ever considered doing sales at a gym?

That, literally, is what I said. Now, at that point, I still thought my idea was a great one as we are always looking for great talent. Once I said that and without hesitation the gentleman says:

"I think you should try this special sea salt lotion from the Dead Sea."

In other words, totally disregarding what I asked him and just moving right into sales mode. What seemed like a great idea crashed and burned within five seconds. So I thought to myself, what a terrible idea and I decided that I was going to cut my losses and walk away. As I had that thought I noticed the other salesman working that kiosk walking toward me. By this time there are now two salesmen in front of me and the one that walked over asks:

"Do you get manicures"?

Now I will admit, I wasn't sure why he asked that question and the even more baffling part to that was why I replied:

"Yes I do"

Why didn't I just walk away? Was it pride to the fact that I didn't want to give in and say no and have him think that I don't take care of my nails? So after I had given in and said yes, the original salesman takes out what looks like a small nail file and starts buffering my one nail on my ring finger. Now if you could, picture me in the middle of the mall with two guys in front of me and one is buffering my nail. What the hell is going on? So ten seconds of buffering goes by and he shows me my one nail. The most amazing thing happened. My nail looked AWESOME. To put it into perspective I want to tell you how awesome it looked. It was so shiny that for a split second, I actually felt bad for the other nine fingernails. Can you imagine being the one shiny fingernail when the other nine looked like they were homeless? He proceeded to tell me the price of the buffer and for a split second I thought about buying it. Now don't worry because I'm not stupid. Of course I didn't buy it but I did think about it.

In my head at this time I was thinking that I'm outta here and I started to walk away. As I'm walking away, though, I can hear one of the guys shouting something to me and as I turn around I see something in the air headed toward me. It was a sample packet of sea salt lotion that the guy threw to me and it was hurdling through the air right at me. Being a great athlete, of course, I catch that packet and thought to myself that at least I would get to try it out. Once again this was a bad idea on my part. Apparently catching that packet gave the guy the right to come back up to me to try and sell me, again, sea salt lotion from the Dead Sea. Now, however, he is trying to sell me not one bottle of lotion but rather a box of four. He also says this:

"This box would be a great Thanksgiving Day present"

Now even though Thanksgiving was one-week away, I remember thinking to myself that I have never given a Thanksgiving Day present to anyone. I mean it is definitely logical to give presents on birthdays and Christmas but NEVER Thanksgiving. Almost in disbelief at this point, I brush the guy off and basically told him thanks but no thanks. Now don't get me wrong, I kept the packet of lotion. This was a turning point in my life, believe it or not, because I remember standing in the middle of the mall and thinking to myself what a horrible sales experience that was. I also remember thinking how I couldn't wait until the next day so I can tell the sales group that I was teaching how never to sell "that" way.

Now if the story ended there it would still be a great story of how not to sell but the story got even better. As I re-organized my thoughts and started walking through the mall again I stumbled upon one of my favorite stores. Now on the outside it says "Foot Locker" but that is not my favorite store. You see inside every Foot Locker there is another store called the "House of Hoops". This is where they keep the more expensive NIKE gear like Michael Jordan and Kevin Durant. That section even has better lighting and the clothes are folded even better. It's for us rich folk you might say. Now since I have worked with NIKE in the past, I like seeing what the latest trends are so I begin to enter the store. As I enter Foot Locker I see the typical sales guy walking toward me about to ask, what every sales guy asks, which was what can I help you with. This time, however, to my dismay he doesn't say that at all. In fact this is what he says:

"Nice NIKE T.R. 4.0 sneakers"

What? Could it be, a sales guy who doesn't ask what can I help you with today? As I did a double take in my mind as to what he just said, I simply replied:

"Thanks man, I can't believe you know the make and the model"

Lets face it; he could have just said "nice kicks". Instead he knew the make and model number of the sneakers I was wearing. The NIKE T.R. 4.0 sneaker was a low profile sneaker that I often like to wear when I am giving sales presentations. I proceed to tell him that I work for a gym chain and when I teach the sales people I like to be comfortable. The T.R. 4.0 is the most comfortable sneaker that I like to wear. Now as I am telling him this he looks at me and says:

"I actually workout all the time"

At which point his friends start to break out in laughter. I, obviously, ask why his friends were laughing? At that point his friend's say:

"He works out but does chest every day of the week"

Typical guy right? Chest workouts Monday-Friday used to be the old me. So we all start laughing and have a conversation about where he is working out now and why he has never been to the gym I work for. I proceed to tell the group that if I can get some guest passes for my gym would you use them. Of course the answer was yes, so I made a call to some sales advisors and told them to come in tomorrow to give these employees some passes. So what does this part of the story have to do with anything? The answer is everything because after about ten minutes with these guys the sales guy casually points to a rack and says:

"Just so you know, buy eight socks and get eight for free"

Is this a dream I thought? Could it be that if I buy eight socks I can get eight pairs for free. So I did what any sane man would do and I bought the eight socks. I also forgot to mention that I do not need any socks and that's when it hit me. I walked out of the store with sixteen pairs of socks, stood in the middle of the mall and thought this very thought:

"Why did I not buy something I actually wanted (nail buffer) but bought something I actually didn't need (socks)"?

This story has molded the way I think about sales to this day. It taught me that the most powerful tool a sales person or company can create is a great experience. I told you earlier that what I do is try not to sell. If you think about the two different experiences I had at the mall you will understand that there was no rapport building at the lotion kiosk. The only thing the lotion kiosk salesmen wanted to do was sell me Sea Salt Lotion from the Dead Sea or a nail buffer. The difference was that it took almost ten minutes for anyone in the Foot Locker store to point out anything in the actual store. We built a relationship first talking about working out and didn't spend time talking about what Foot Locker sells. I felt so comfortable in that situation that it was ok for me to buy sixteen pairs of socks. So this brings me back to "Why" I go to Starbucks, twice a day, to buy a two dollar and forty cents coffee. Let's look at the experience I get when I walk into a Starbucks.

Whenever I walk into a Starbucks the first thing I notice and feel is the element of calm and accomplishment. When you look around you see everyday people sitting and either typing on their laptops or talking on their phones. All of these people are getting things done in their lives. Whether it is working on a term paper for school, finishing a presentation for work or just scouring the web for true love, they are all getting things done. This is astounding to me because they are all accomplishing this in a coffee shop.

As I get to the counter what you will always notice is that the Barista (because that's what we call them) are never on their phones. Now before I move on I really want you to think about what I just said. That's right NEVER on their phones. It is amazing, plain and simple. Almost anywhere you go usually you will find an employee in a store texting someone or better yet, posting something on Facebook and yet that doesn't go on in Starbucks. I then magically speak Italian in Starbucks even though I have never taken Italian classes because I say things like "Venti Macchiato" or "Grande Pike". The Barista then asks me my name and writes it on the cup, however, what's notable is that they even ask how you spell your name. I mean let's be honest you can just quickly hear my name, Kory, and write it a few different ways and yet the Barista takes the time to make sure it's spelled correctly: K-O-R-Y. The best part about this entire experience is that when I do get my coffee, although not the best in the world, it always tastes the same. In other words, the experience is always consistent. This is "The Starbucks Effect". They have effectively taken the word "disappointment" out of my vocabulary every time I walk into one of their establishments.

That is truly amazing. Ponder for a second and ask yourself; is there a place you frequent where you can truly say you are never disappointed?

Think about the words value proposition. Essentially, can you get to the point where a customer values your product so much that they, not only are willing to spend money, but even more money for that very same product.

Do you get the point? If you do not understand after reading the above then that means you suck at sales. Sorry, your just average at sales if it makes you feel any better. The troubling part for me is most sales people do not see why they are just average.

So here is what it comes down to:

QUESTION:

"Why do I drink a $2.40 coffee from Starbucks twice a day?"

ANSWER:

"Because it is not about the coffee"

Now that you understand what "The Starbucks Effect" is, let's take a look at where creating a great experience ranks in a sales process. For this we are going to look at a study by Club Industry. Club Industry is one of the leading health and fitness magazines around today.

There was a survey done by Club Industry in August of 2009 that looked at the top reasons a person joins a health club. The top reasons are listed in figure 4:

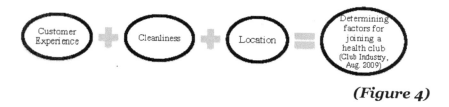

(Figure 4)

When I looked at the results of this survey I instantly understood what "The Starbucks Effect" was and how powerful a great customer experience could be. I immediately noticed that price was not in the top three. When I ask most people what you think the number one reason is for joining a particular gym, the answer is usually the price. I mean it sounds like common sense that someone would join a gym based on the cheapest deal. To that point, even if it weren't the number one reason surely price would come in at number two. To my surprise it wasn't the second reason either. In fact, when you really look at this survey what you gather from it is that someone is willing to pay more money to join a gym as long as they get a great customer experience, it is clean and it is close to home. That is crazy right? Whether it's joining a gym, buying coffee or leasing a car, creating a great experience is the most important part in getting a sale.

> 66
>
> ***"Starbucks represents something beyond a cup of coffee"***
> -Howard Schultz
>
> 99

CHAPTER 4

Climbing The Sales Ladder

I BELIEVE THAT you are either great at sales or you are just average. What makes a great salesman is the ability to build rapport resulting in a great experience. You also can't talk about value proposition without talking about building rapport. You see rapport is the key in any sales relationship. If you dig into the weeds with most sales people you will find that the reason they are doing an average job is because they lack or do not take the time to build a relationship with a customer. What most people think about is just making the sale. Value is hard to build without rapport; in fact they go hand in hand.

So let us talk about the "SALES WALL" first. By "SALES WALL" I mean the very feeling someone gets when a sales person either walks up to him or her or calls him or her on the phone. Let me show you what I mean. Walk into any store and likely you will find a sales person that approaches you and says the following:

"Can I help you with anything?"

Now of course you already know what nine out of ten humans reply with:

"No thanks, I am just looking"

Yes, that is the "SALES WALL" I am talking about. Now this happens because everywhere we go we are presented with average sales people who within the first five seconds try to sell you something. The ironic part is that we can probably use the help more often than not. Before we talk about how to build rapport and how that leads to a more comfortable sales experience, lets take a look at what rapport really means.

Definition: **Rapport-**

A close and harmonious relationship in which the people or groups concerned understands each other's feelings or ideas and communicates well. (Source: Wikipedia)

We think, as sales people that we do a great job of building rapport. We ask questions, therefore, assume we must be doing a great job of relationship building. I am here to tell you though that, that is not the case. In fact, I call it the FAKE RAPPORT SYMDROME (FRS).

Definition: **Fake Rapport Syndrome (FRS)-**

The art of building a fake rapport with someone. (Source: Kory Angelin)

For example, I have been a part of many companies where they teach you to start out with a compliment. I mean if the goal is to not start off by selling your product or idea what better way to start out a conversation than with a compliment. The FRS effect, however, is when you might start out with a compliment but it is really just a fake one. Almost as if you wanted to fill up some space until ten seconds later when you want to start selling that person your product or service. There's no greater example of this than a sales advisor at a gym. One of their jobs, in addition to selling gym memberships, is to get leads. Leads are people that might be interested in using a guest pass to try out the gym. Very often you will see sales advisors at a mall or a high traffic area handing out guest passes. Here is where you get a good look at FRS first hand. A person walks by and the sales advisor might stop that person and say:

"I love your shirt"

Obviously it is a compliment intended to get a person to stop for a minute. The problem with FRS is that once you say that compliment, the next statement usually heard from the sales advisor is:

"So would you like a three day guest pass for my gym?"

In other words you spent one sentence complimenting a persons shirt and then moved right on to what you wanted to sell that person, which in this case is a guest pass. That is what I mean by Fake Rapport Syndrome. Your compliment really did not mean anything in the context of the conversation. To really build rapport you need to invest in understanding the persons needs and wants. When I think about how effective building rapport can be as it relates to the sales process I think about the sales ladder. The sales ladder, if done correctly, is the most effective way to come out with a result, whether it is a lead or a sale.

Another important factor to remember is that a result doesn't necessarily mean that you get a sale in that moment. We will discuss what result can mean as we go through the steps of the ladder (figure 5: The Sales ladder).

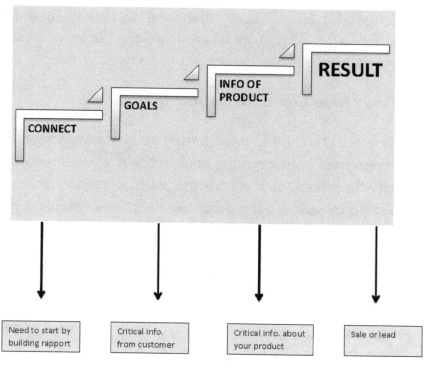

(Figure 5: The Sales Ladder)

1. CONNECT:

The first step in any sales cycle should be to connect with an individual on a personal level. Previously we talked about how a true compliment can be very effective in sales. Most sales people do not do a good job at connecting which is why most people "suck" at sales. You can't climb the sales ladder unless you get past connecting so, in most cases, "connecting" is the most important step of the ladder. Here is how effective connecting is in building rapport.

I was recently in Virginia teaching a group of sales advisors as part of a two-day course. Since I was there for two days I decided to go to the mall after day one had ended to shop around a bit, as well as, to kill some time. I ended up walking into an Oakley store where I noticed the saleswoman approaching me. She came right up to me and said:

"Can I help you with anything?"

Of course I thought to myself, what an idiot for saying that. I mean hasn't she read my book yet? Why would you say that? Stop being like every other sales person where you start off by selling something. So after those thoughts entered my head I simply said:

"No thank you, I am just looking"

So I walk around and ended up at a table where there was some shirts nicely folded. The woman approaches me again and says:

"I like your shirt, that is one of ours right?"

Sure enough I was wearing an Oakley golf shirt with the name of the gym I work for embroidered onto the chest. She proceeds to say how she loves that style shirt because it's the new dri-fit material. She also asks if I work for the health club that is on my shirt. Of course I say yes and that turns into me finding out where she currently works out, what her goals were and why she is trying to achieve those goals. Her goal was to lose eighteen pounds because she has a wedding coming up in three months and she is in the wedding party. I would say we spent about ten minutes talking about different ways to reach her goal, as well as, talking about the benefits of coming to my gym in that area since she has never been there. In other words we did not talk about anything that she was selling. There was no "everything in the store is 25% off" or "buy 2 shirts get another one 50% off". The end result was that I walked out of the store having purchased two Oakley shirts.

When I looked back at why I bought something when I had no intention of doing so, I came to the conclusion that because she connected with me in a different way than when I first walked in, I felt more comfortable and was willing to lower my "SALES WALL". If you cant connect with someone, then every other ring of the ladder becomes that much harder. Remember Fake Rapport Syndrome (FRS), if you're going to connect or compliment someone, make it real.

2. GOALS

Once you get passed connecting with someone you then get to one of the hardest parts of the sales ladder which is to understand the needs and wants of the person. Understanding someone's goals sounds easy but, in fact, it is the place where most sales people fail. What everyone should understand is that the only reason why someone would want what your selling is to reach his or her own personal goal. For example, let us take a look at the fitness industry where someone's goal is the most important thing. Think about why a person would not only use a guest pass at a gym but also join the gym and maybe even spend money to work with a trainer. There is only one reason why they would do that and the answer is to reach their fitness goal. That is everything in the fitness world and yet most sales people either barely talk about the person's goal or sometimes never touch upon it at all. If you don't understand someone's goals then how could you expect them to buy what you are selling?

Let us take a look at an example of a sales advisor at a gym who's job it is to get a person to use a guest pass and then join the gym. One task a sales advisor does on a daily basis is to make phone calls to potential people who might want to use a guest pass. Here's how the call typically goes:

"Hi Jon, this is Steve from _____ . I wanted to see if you wanted to activate your guest pass to try out our gym?"

And there it is, the very reason why most people suck at

sales. Steve, in this example, took all of five seconds to give out what he is selling. He actually missed the "connect" step entirely and went right to trying to give something out. Here's the problem, we talked previously that a persons goal is the very reason why someone would even use a guest pass at a gym and then go on to join it. Yet, in this example Steve did not even bring up anything having to do with Jon's goals. For a sales person to understand someone's goals, you actually have to ask. The call should go like this:

"Hi Jon, this is Steve from _____ . I got your name from your brother Chris who just joined our gym. He said you might want to come and experience the gym as well but I would love to take 30 seconds just to find out what your fitness goal is and how its been going in trying to reach it."

If you think about it, every call should be wrapped around the needs and wants of the person and not what you have to give out. Don't get me wrong; the end result is to give out what you have to sell but take the time to understand why a person would want that in the first place. I always tell sales people, how can you give a solution if you do not understand what the person's problem is in the first place. If you remember the Sea Salt Hand Lotion from earlier, it took less than five seconds for the salesman to try and sell me the lotion. It happens in every experience I have with sales people.

I recently got a knock on my door at six p.m. in the evening.

The first thought that goes through my mind is the fact that someone is knocking at six p.m. in the evening. I already know it's a sales person trying to sell something. So I proceed to answer the door and encounter a woman with a solar roofing company shirt on. They were scouring the neighborhood, knocking on peoples doors to see if families were interested in installing solar panels on their roofs. Now, do not get me wrong but this has always intrigued me. I would hear stories that the installation is free and can save thousands on your electric bill down the road. I could have actually been interested in what she had to say but then "it" happened. She was like the rest of the average sales people in the world. This was her opening line:

"Hi, my name is Karen and I wanted to see if you were interested in solar panels"?

Are you kidding me? There is no difference between that and a sales advisor at a gym asking if I wanted to activate a guest pass. Talk about not even making an effort to connect with me. This, however, is what happens all the time. My belief is that most sales people do not have the right amount of training and coaching. It is why "The Big 3", discussed earlier, is so important in a sales job. The most important thing a solar panel sales person should want to know is why I would want solar panels. When you fail to understand my goals for wanting solar panels you miss the point entirely. Building rapport and connecting make it easier to understand the needs and wants of a customer.

What if her opening line was:

"Hi, my name is Karen and I wanted to know if you wanted to hear about how you can save lots of money every month on your electric bill."

Finding out someone's needs and wants also requires the ability to **listen.** Now, I know what you are thinking, how can someone not listen. So, for those of you that do not believe me when I tell you that humans are really bad at listening, I will prove it to you. Has, at any time in your life, your significant other said to you that you don't listen? You know when you are watching television, your spouse tells you something and you only remember half of what they said. If you're reading this and saying to yourself that that has never happened to me, then you are lying. It used to happen to me all the time. I would meet someone, we would introduce ourselves and fifteen minutes later I would forget his/her name. The human brain works in such a way that when you ask someone a question, we immediately are thinking what to say next. What this means is that we move from being present in the moment to the future because that very thing you're thinking about saying hasn't happened yet. This phenomenon happens all of the time.

One of my favorite skill builders when I teach is all about active listening. I pair the group up into two's and I tell them that one person is going to talk about something they are very passionate about for sixty seconds. I then tell the group that for the sixty seconds your partner is talking, I DO NOT want you to listen. Once they get over laughing as if I was joking they thought about how they are going to do that. So during the exercise you see how uncomfortable it is to, not only speak for sixty seconds without the other person paying attention, but also to intentionally not listen. That is what happens everyday because even though I told them not to listen, they can still hear part of what the other person is saying. The problem, however, is that they just cant process all of the information. Listening is a key characteristic to have if you truly want to understand a person's needs and wants.

3. INFORMATION OF THE PRODUCT

Okay so let us say you did a good job at connecting with someone and understanding what the person's goals are, you absolutely need to know the information of your own product. You would be surprised at how many sales people do not know everything about their product or service. I am talking about knowing your product inside and out because what most sales people do is show people pricing sheets. That is the kiss of death and here's why. Let's say I was talking with you right now and we are talking about my gym that I work for. In the middle of me talking to you I pull out a sheet with all of the pricing options on it. So, although you might be listening to me, part of your concentration will start to focus on the sheet of paper that is in front of your face. Knowing everything about your product or service ensures that you will be more conversational with a potential buyer.

There is something special when someone pays full attention to what you're saying; so knowing your product inside and out is extremely important. Right now, if you can't recite everything about your product that you sell then you need to do some homework and study. I recently helped my wife car shop because her current lease was up. Anyone that knows me knows that I used to walk into car dealerships to see what "not" to do when it comes to selling. The mere words "car salesmen" has several negative connotations attached to it. I very often wonder though how that came to be. I mean when cars were first invented, the number one sales job in America had to be selling cars. So somewhere between when cars were first invented until now there was a massive transition of how car salesman go about selling that product. In fact, most car salesman skip the connect part of the sales ladder completely. They go right to:

"So what are you interested in today?"

My wife and I happened to walk into one dealership where the sales guy had to keep getting up to ask his manager what other fees were attached to the deal they were offering us. Obviously, I decided not to lease a car from him. Know your product because it is the easiest part of the sales ladder to learn. The information is there but you just have to take the time to learn it. When it comes to information about your product sometimes I use, what I like to call, "up sell/ down sell". I learned it when I was selling heart rate monitors and learned that it could be used in any sales situation and with any product or service. So here's an example of what this technique is all about.

Let us say I am wearing a five hundred dollar heart rate monitor so when I exercise I can keep track of what zone I am in. Many high-end gyms actually sell a variety of heart rate monitor watches because of the popularity of them. Heart rate monitor watches can range from fifty to five hundred dollars in stores. "Up sell to down sell" technique would sound something like this:

"So you definitely need a heart rate monitor watch like we talked about earlier. I'm wearing a $500 one but the good news is that you don't need one this fancy. You can get away with one that's only $200".

Now, if I just started saying that you need a two hundred dollar heart rate monitor then that would sound expensive because it's the only price I mentioned. Two hundred dollars is the only seed that I planted in that situation. The fact, however, that I mentioned five hundred dollars first and that you do not need that watch made the two hundred dollar price more appealing. I find that this is such an underutilized tool in the sales industry. This is why outlet stores are so popular. Walk into any outlet store and you will see an items original cost on the price tag with the reduced price under it. So what catches your eye first is an item that was originally marked one hundred and fifty-dollars but under it says outlet price is seventy-five dollars. What a bargain right? I bet you though that if you walked into a store and saw an item for seventy five-dollars with no reduction that you would think that was a lot of money-"Up sell/down sell". Car dealers, although lack connecting with the customer, actually use the "up sell/ down sell" technique quite often. You will always be told the MSRP (Manufacturer's Sales Retail Price) on the car that you are interested in. Once you have that number in mind the dealer will tell you that he/she got a great deal and that their price is lower than that number. So not only knowing the information of your own product is important but also understanding how to use that to your advantage.

4. RESULT

Having the right ingredients can help create a great result. It is what I like to call "The Success Martini" (see figure 6: The Success Martini).

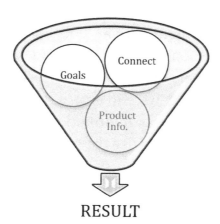

RESULT

(Figure 6: The Success Martini)

Result is one of the most misunderstood concepts in the sales ladder because we immediately think that it means making a sale. This, however, isn't always the case and should not always be the expectation. I tell people all of the time that although your mindset should be that you will close every deal you are in front of, reality dictates that that is impossible. Do not mistake how powerful making a great connection and giving a great experience is. Making a sale does not always have to happen right then and there, in fact, many times the sale happens days or weeks later.

I remember when I worked at a gym in NY City. It was at their Wall Street location where so many of the members were stockbrokers. Most of these stockbrokers did not have time to take a tour of the club prior to them joining. They just wanted to get the price of how much it costs to join and then make a quick decision. My strategy, however, never changes in that I believe the most important action in sales is to give someone a great experience, whether that takes ten minutes or an hour. So that is what I did and often a person left having not made a decision on joining or not. When someone was interested in pricing right away and said they were in a rush, I started out by trying to find out one piece of information, which was what area of the gym, they would use the most. It sounded like this:

"So before I tell you the price, if you were a member here, what one area of the gym would you use the most?

After I asked this question the most amazing thing happened-they actually told me what area they were most interested in. Why was this so critical? Well, this is a person who started out by saying that they don't really have time for anything like a tour and just wanted to know the price. What ended up happening is once they told me what they were interested in, it evolved into a tour.

"So since the cardio section is the area you would use the most, lets walk over there while we talk about pricing."

Getting someone to walk with you on a tour is so critical in the fitness industry because that turns into building a connection and breaks down the sales wall that the customer has. Most people, in fact, are in a rush or at least that's what they say. So whether you are in a gym or walk into a store in the mall, reality is that people are expecting you to try and sell them something. In dealing with this type of person at a gym, my expectation is not to sell them a membership that day but simply to give a person what they want. In that case, it happens to be pricing while showing them what they would actually be using as a member. I mean lets face it, I don't care who you are but anyone joining a gym would at least like to see the one area they would be using the most. Building a great experience was my only goal and as a result many of those customers walked away with a guest pass to try the gym out. So although the experience did not result in a sale that day it did, many times, result in a sale a few days later. Many of those customers that used the guest pass appreciated that I did not try to sell them on a gym membership the day they came in. In return, those customers came back after they were done using the pass and joined with me.

One of the best fitness professionals I know used to tell me that most of his sales came days or weeks after he put the time into building a connection. What he would do while he was training one of his clients was to make it a point to always say hi to the members around him. It, sometimes, could be a quick hello or a little bit more involved depending upon how much time he had. The lesson from this is actually pretty profound because days, weeks and sometimes even months later, some of those members decided that they would consider using a trainer to reach their goals. Of course, whom do you think they turned to? You see he could have done what most sales people do and that is to walk up to someone in the gym and say something like this:

"Hi, did you do your fitness consultation yet?

I know, it sounds pretty innocent and it's actually not bad. What your not realizing is that even though the question was a good one, there is no connection between him and the member. The member still has that wall up because within the first five seconds my friend was essentially trying to sell something. Now imagine if you will my friend spending a few weeks having small conversations with that same member. Planting seeds throughout those weeks about how effective it could be to work with a trainer. The trainer might even show the member one or two exercises to do on their own. Now, fast-forward a few weeks when my friend decides to walk up to the member and say:

"By the way, did you take advantage of your free fitness consultation? If you haven't, lets do it"

Almost all of the members that he did this with ended up, not only doing the assessment, but also purchased a training package from him. As long as you are able to follow the steps in the Sales ladder your result has a better chance of ending up in a sale. Sales people need to really think about not sounding desperate because if it feels like your being desperate, chances are that you are. Here is an example of how some sales people sound desperate.

I walked into a furniture store recently and, of course, was swarmed by five guys in suits. Nothing new there so I ended up talking with one of the men and expressed to him that I was just looking around at some couches. We walked around and tried some of the couches in the store. He proceeded to tell me that there were some amazing holiday sales going on if I acted today. Now get ready, as I'm sure you have never heard this before, the salesman says:

"This is the last day of the sale so I just want to let you know that if you don't buy this couch today, I cant guarantee this price later".

Ugh, say it isn't so, did he just really use that line on me? To me it is just a ridiculous and desperate line used by most average sales people. I felt like really saying that if I came back in two days, I am sure you can offer the same price to me. Okay so if you don't believe that example look no further than "Black Friday".

If there is one day where sales people have fooled the consumer it is "Black Friday". Imagine waking up at three a.m.

to go to Best Buy, only to wait in line for hours until they open. Hundreds of dollars off televisions for that one day, so you better get their early they say. This day has baffled me and intrigued me all at the same time. My sister is one of those people that gets up at three a.m. and waits on the Best Buy line. She will say it is worth it because she can save a hundred dollars on a television so that becomes the motivation to do it. What I really believe is that there is some adrenaline rush built around that day. Excitement that you will be buying something and that you are getting a great deal on it. This, however, is where I find Black Friday interesting.

This past Black Friday I, like many other consumers, did not go near the retail stores. There is no way that I want to be part of the "herd" that bum rushes the store to save a penny. That following Sunday, however, I was re-arranging my son's room and decided that he needed a new television. Of course my thought was to go to Best Buy because it happens to be around the corner. That is when I realized how Black Friday is the only day where the retail stores have fooled the consumer. As I sauntered on in to Best Buy I made a beeline to the televisions in the back. My first impression was that the store was not crowded. I found that interesting given that Black Friday was two days prior. As I arrived in that section I noticed signs on every television, which said:

25% OFF ALL T.V.'S

Same price as on *Black Friday*

As I studied all of the signs posted on top of the televisions I thought to myself that I couldn't believe the prices were exactly the same on Sunday as they were on Black Friday. How could that be? Black Friday is the one-day a year where you get the best deal and you are just out of luck if you can't make it there that day. At least that is what my sister and a million other people think on that day. People believe that Black Friday is the one-day a year where they will be getting the best price. It is desperation on that day to make it to your favorite retail store. I, however, was having the last laugh. Once I called my sister to gloat for a bit, I walked out of Best Buy that day with a brand new television for the same price that it was on Friday.

When you think about results and how it is the last part of the sales ladder, think more in terms of how productive that interaction was with the customer. Productivity is a far better way to think about results in sales than an actual sale. At the end of the day, if you made a great connection with a customer by following all of the steps of the sales ladder, I believe that was a productive result and interaction. Don't rely on sales and promos to make a sale. Even if the customer does not purchase anything that day, the likelihood of them seeing you again is much greater. Very often sales isn't viewed in that prism. It is simply how many opportunities did you have that day versus how many sales you made. Sales, however, is not that cut and dry. Take a look at two statistics about customers who visit car dealerships for the first time.

> **72% of customers tell their salesperson they are "just looking" at the initial greeting.**
> (Source: Joe Verde Group, Nada Studies)

> **71% of customers say they bought their vehicle because they like, trusted and respected their salesperson.**
> (Source: Joe Verde Group, Nada Studies)

About seven out of every ten customers tell a car dealer that they are "just looking" on the initial visit. Which means, ultimately, that only three customers are actually making a deal to buy a car. So the question is- was the experience so good for the seven that did not buy, that they would end up coming back after shopping other dealers? If the answer is no, then you are not climbing the sales ladder efficiently. This is why looking at a result in a few different ways is important.

If you look, however, at the second statistic it simply proves the point that a great experience can result in a sale now or later. Seven out of every ten customers ended up purchasing the vehicle simply because they trusted and respected their salesperson. Notice it does not say because of price, although that is a factor. We talked earlier, however, how customers are willing to spend more money as long as they get a great experience.

Remember that each rung of the sales ladder affects the next one. Truly being great at sales means you are great at each one. Since each one depends on the success of the other, do not take for granted how important it is to analyze every sales encounter you have. Look into what went right and what you could have done differently. If you can do this, you can make sure you do not repeat the same habits over and over again.

CHAPTER 5

Ask and Overcome

ASKING FOR THE SALE:

LET'S RECAP. So far we talked about the fact that people do not buy a product unless they believe in its result. Furthermore, we learned how building a rapport could lead to a better connection with a guest. Once you build that connection you are creating a value to the product you are selling. Once there is value in a product or service, your percent of making a sale increases two-fold.

One of the biggest areas of concern for any sales person comes right at the end. I am sure you know what I am talking about. Yes, having to actually ask for the sale. We talked earlier about one of my favorite statistics:

#1 reason why someone does not make a sale?

They don't ask

I know it's always shocking anytime I read that but that doesn't make it less true. The fact is, most people tense up when it comes time to ask for money. The biggest reason for this is how money is viewed from the sales person's point of view. In other words, because the sales person thinks that the amount of money they are asking for is a lot, they believe that it is a lot for the customer too. Here's a simple example.

A personal trainer, as discussed previously, is tasked with getting customer's to buy thousand dollar-training packages. Sometimes a twenty four-session package with a trainer could be around fourteen hundred dollars. That amount of money, like with most of us, seems like a lot, therefore, when they ask for that amount of money from the customer they are nervous. Sometimes they actually do, what I like to call, "word salad". This is where a sales person starts talking in circles and mixing a lot of words together because they are afraid to actually ask for the sale. We have all been there before. There is nothing more powerful, however, than being confident in sales. It's a trait that is hard to teach. If a trainer truly believes that by purchasing a twenty four-session training package with him/her could potentially change the customer's life for the better, then why wouldn't you be confident in asking? Sounds easy of course but I learned over the years that for you to be confident in asking for a sale, you must be confident in what you are selling.

There is no doubt in my mind that if someone trains with me to reach a fitness goal, they will reach it. Partly because of what we are going to do in the gym together and partly because I am going to hold them accountable when they are not at the gym. I believe that if we take that journey together that you will see results. It is because of that result that I am more than confident in the money I charge for personal training. When you hear me ask for the sale, you better believe that I believe it is worth the money.

So, obviously, we know that asking for the sale is essential in actually making one. There is, however, a secret to asking for a sale. When traveling a few weeks ago, I decided to go to a nearby restaurant to my hotel for dinner. Very often I like to ask the waiter or waitress what they recommend on the menu. I like to use this example because it is relatable to each and every one of us at some point. Whether it is a waiter, waitress or bartender, we often ask their opinion as to what stands out on the menu. The first task was to figure out what kind of food I was in the mood for and for me it was a salad. I glanced at all seven salads and tried to figure out which one I liked the best. At that point the waitress came by to see if I was ready to order. I looked at her and said:

"What salad do you recommend?"

She pointed to the menu and said:

"The grilled chicken avocado salad"

Now, I know what you are thinking. What does this have to do with asking for the sale? This, however, has everything to do with it. You see before I told the waitress that I was going to get the grilled chicken avocado salad that she recommended, I wanted to know one more piece of critical information. So I looked up and said:

"Why do you recommend that one"?

Without hesitation the waitress said:

"Because the avocado is fresh"

SOLD- to the gentleman named Kory. We talked in Chapter one how the "Why" is the most critical component in sales. Understanding the "Why" allows you to put all of the pieces together so you can figure out if that product or service is of value to you. The "Why" here was that the avocado was fresh and who doesn't love fresh avocado. I started to think about the power of recommendation when it's coupled with a reason. The best way to teach someone how to effectively ask for a sale is to learn "The Arrow Ask" (See Figure 7: The Arrow Ask).

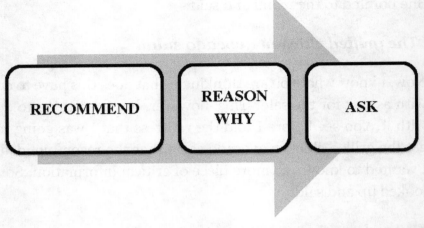

(Figure 7: The Arrow Ask)

Although the above illustration is a very simple one, it really captures how to be effective in sales. Let us breakdown each of these three components and see why, when combined, is a powerful tool in building value in a product or service.

1. Recommend:

Why is it more powerful to make a recommendation when asking for a sale versus leaving it up to the customer as to which option they would want? Earlier we talked about the one component that is hardest to teach which is confidence. You have to be confident with your product or service in sales. No one wants to purchase a service or product from a sales person who is not confident in what they are selling. Confidence is a re-assurance to the customer that you believe in the product. Therefore, when it comes time to ask for the sale you should be confident in making a recommendation as to what you think the customer should purchase. The reason for this is simple; you are the expert.

If I was to ask a bartender what drink they recommend, I am assuming that he/she has been doing this for a while and probably has a great opinion as to what is a good drink. This simple concept transcends to any business situation. You never leave a decision up to a customer because most of the time they need help making the decision.

In the fitness industry we call our sales people sales advisors. The reason for this is because we want to empower them to advise customers as to the best membership type they think the customer should purchase. The sales advisor is also an expert at understanding what the gym offers and how the different membership types work. You would never hear a sales advisor say:

"So out of these 5 membership types, which one would you like to do"?

The customer, in that situation, has information overload on a subject that he/she are not experts on. I compare this to when you paint a room in your house and you are trying to decide on a paint color. When deciding on a color, the sales person at Home Depot pulls out the swath of color samples. I would rather him/her recommend a particular color than just hand it to me and say which one of these thousand colors would you want. The more effective way a sales advisor should ask for the sale is by saying:

"So based on all of your goals we talked about and the fact that you know you will be committed to coming to the gym for the next year, I

would recommend you go with the commitment membership".

This is more effective because it steers the customer to a specific option. It also shows that the sales advisor has an understanding about the goals of the customer, which helps in making a recommendation.

2. Why

Although making a confident recommendation when asking for the sale is important, it is truly not effective unless you give a reason "Why". We talked in length about how "The Golden Circle" teaches us that the "Why" is what customers care about. Answer the "Why" and you are more likely to get buy in from the customer. Let us use the above example of a sales advisor asking for the sale but let's also add in a reason why. The reason why we are going to use is a price reason. Although I believe that price isn't the true issue for a customer saying no, I realize we are all focused on price as sales people. This was what the sales advisor said earlier:

Reason Why

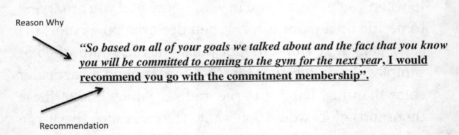

"So based on all of your goals we talked about and the fact that you know you will be committed to coming to the gym for the next year, I would recommend you go with the commitment membership".

Recommendation

Clearly, the sales advisor gave a recommendation and gave a reason why they were recommending the commitment membership type. The reason for that is that the customer stated that he/she was committed to reaching their fitness goal over the course of the next year. Since the commitment membership is a yearlong membership, the sales advisor used that as a reason why. People that excel at sales not only recommend with confidence but also give multiple reasons why the customer should say yes. So how do you take the above comment from a sales advisor at a gym and make it even more effective? So a sales advisor does a great job giving the customer a tour of their gym. They spent the hour building rapport, which in turn, builds value in the product. In this case, the value is in a membership at this particular gym. The sales advisor sits down with the potential member and says this:

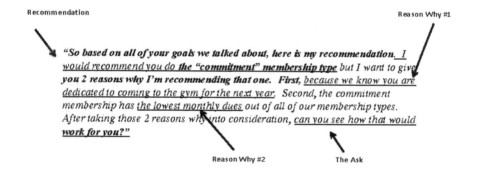

3. The Ask

There is nothing more effective than making a confident recommendation along with multiple reasons why the customer should say yes. There is, however, one important but often-overlooked component to the above statement. You actually have to ask for the sale. Many times I hear a great, confident recommendation along with a reason why and then no "ask". Here was my ask from the above example:

", can you see how that would work for you?"

Without that line, there would be awkward silence. Your ask might be different depending upon what field you are in but it has to be there. It is hard to get buy in from the customer without all of these components. Let us go back to the example I used when I ordered a grilled chicken avocado salad. What was the reason why the waitress recommended that particular salad? The reason was because of the fresh avocado. Now I will say she could have made that even more effective if she said:

"I would recommend the grilled chicken avocado salad because the avocado is super fresh. Can you see how that would work for you?"

That one statement has all of the components of the "Arrow Ask" and happens to be the reason I chose that particular salad. The "ask" should also be a "Closed Ended Question" and not an "Open-Ended" one. Let us take a look at the difference between the two.

OPEN-ENDED QUESTIONS:

An open-ended question allows the respondent to answer in any way they choose.

Although open-ended questions work well in building rapport, the biggest drawback to these questions happen when its time to ask for a sale. The reason for that is because when it is time to ask for a sale, you want to make it as easy as possible for a customer to say yes. Here are some in-effective ways for a sales advisor at a gym to ask for a sale using "Open-Ended Questions":

1. *"Which of the several membership options we have to offer would you be interested in?"*

2. *"Out of the multiple options we have, which one would you like to buy?"*

These examples are open-ended questions, which have less impact than closed ended do. The more you leave a sale open ended, the more a buyer can ponder a variety of answers and possibilities.

CLOSED-ENDED QUESTIONS:

A closed ended question is a question, whereby; the respondent has to give a "yes" or a "no".

The reason why a closed ended question is so powerful when asking for a sale is because you're making the choice a simple one. So how would you take the above questions and make them more closed-ended? Here are two examples:

1. *"Can you see how that membership would work for you?"*

2. *"I think that membership would be a great option. How bout we get started today?"*

The less a buyer has to think the more effective you are in guiding them to a decision they, otherwise, could not have made on their own. Furthermore, when you combine a recommendation with a few reasons why and then confidently ask for the sale, you are maximizing your chance of success.

It is time for you to try how easy it is to use the "Arrow Ask". Just plug in whatever your product or service is that you sell and then fill in a reason why someone should purchase it.

**I would recommend _____
_____ and the biggest reason why is because
_____. So can you
see how that can work for you?**

OVERCOMING OBJECTIONS:

It is three p.m. in the afternoon and I see a new email in my inbox. As I open up the message I notice it is from one of our District Managers. This is what the email says:

TO: Kory

FROM: xxxxxx

SUBJECT:

"Hi Kory, I was wondering if you can visit one of my clubs and spend some time with the sales advisors because they are having issues overcoming objections".

Now multiply that email by twenty and you will get an idea of what my inbox looks like. Here's the interesting aspect about this. The first thought someone in my position might have is that the sales team is having trouble overcoming objections. In fact, that is probably the case, however, as you think about that situation the more likely issue is that the sales advisor did not create value in the product, and as a result they got a "no" at the end. Since we spent multiple chapters' talking about how to build value, let's just concentrate on "if" someone says "no" to a sale.

In the following section we are going to learn the four steps in overcoming any objection in sales. Other than asking for the sale, this is the point at which most sales people lose control. They lose control because of one of two reasons.

1. They sound too much like a sales person

2. They get caught off guard and have no process to recover

Saying a sales person sounds too much like a sales person sounds odd but it is the truth. In order to understand this phenomenon in sales, let's take a look at the most common objections in most situations. Here are the top four most common objections:

"I want to think about it"

          "I want to talk to my spouse first"

"It's the price"

          "I want to shop around"

In order for you to understand how to overcome these objections you need to understand which of these four are true. In other words, there is only one real objection out of the four. The only real objection when it comes to sales is the following:

"It's the price"

At the end of the day, if what you were selling were free, you would never hear those other objections. Here is an example of what I mean. Lets pretend that I was asking a customer to buy a gym membership. He/she then turns to me and says:

"I want to think about it but I'll get back to you at some other time"

This, obviously, is a common objection and most sales people would try and overcome that. This, however, isn't the true objection. Hypothetically speaking, what if after the customer says that you reply with the following:

"I totally understand but I forgot to tell you that the gym membership is absolutely free. Do you still need to think about it?"

Of course, the answer would be no because it's free. This is the key to overcoming an objection in that it's always about the price. Therefore, the good news is that you do not need to learn several different ways to overcome several different objections. You just need to learn how to overcome a price objection because that is what it's really about. The other aspect to understand is to stop sounding too much like a sales person. You know that hard core, in your face, intimidating sales person. I know you do not mean to sound like that but the truth is that you do. Here are some examples of what some sales people say when a customer objects.

OBJECTION:
"I want to think about it"

SALES REPLY:
"What is there to think about"?

This isn't a reply that puts a warm fuzzy feeling inside a customer. In fact, when you strip away the ability to show empathy, you have effectively lost trust with the customer.

OBJECTION:
"It's the cost"

SALES REPLY:
"Well, you told me you like to eat out every weekend. If you didn't do that you can afford this"

The minute you tell a customer they can't do something that they love, you have effectively lost the sale. No one wants to hear what he or she can't do.

OBJECTION:
"I need to talk with my wife first"

SALES REPLY:
"Do you want me to step out while you give her a call?"

This is my favorite one out of them all and yet many of us actually say this. This is one of the most disrespectful replies that I hear. Putting someone in this situation is not increasing your odds at making a sale.

Now that you understand what not to do when someone objects, let's show you how having a sound process can help. Once you understand the four steps to overcoming objections, you can then use that process in almost any sales situation.

4 STEPS TO OVERCOMING OBJECTIONS

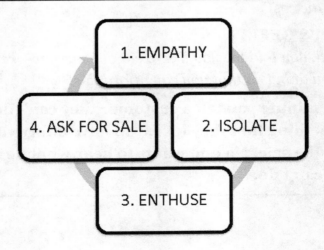

1. EMPATHY

4. ASK FOR SALE

2. ISOLATE

3. ENTHUSE

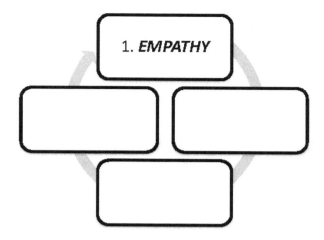

- Let the customer know that you understand that making a decision is difficult.

- Empathy can build trust with the customer.

- Helps to form an emotional bond.

- Makes you part of "their" team and separates you from just being a salesman.

"I completely understand, sometimes making this type of decision can be very difficult."

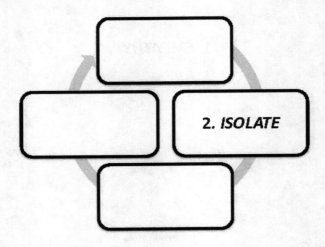

- In order to give a solution, you need to understand the problem.
- Isolate the true reason why they are objecting.
- Never answer an objection.
- Isolating a problem usually comes down to a specific price that you mentioned earlier.

"I just want to make sure I understand what it is that you're struggling with. Is it the specific price?"

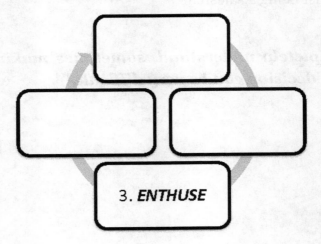

- Get the customer excited again about why they came in today.

- Always keep the customers goal at the forefront.

- Re-enthusing a customer takes their mind off the objection.

"So first, I want to make sure that you are still excited about the prospect of purchasing a...?"

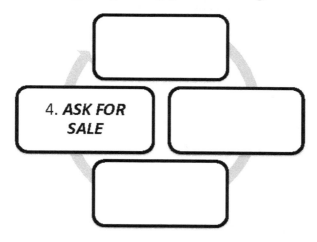

4. ASK FOR SALE

- Asking for a sale more than once is very common.

- You only ask for the sale again once you have completed the prior 3 steps.

- The 3 steps ensures that when you ask again, you are coming up with an alternative option that fits the customers needs but is still sensitive to their objection.

"Since your still excited about your goals, why don't we find you a better option that is less expensive? Would that work for you?"

When you use this process it not only makes overcoming an objection easier but also makes it fun. The reason for this is because you are not stressed out that you need to battle with the customer. What you are really doing is giving the customer a solution to their problem. Here is how all four steps are put together. The example I will use is that of a person possibly looking to buy a gym membership. Now at this point the customer has done a tour with the sales advisor and they then go and sit down at the advisor's desk to talk membership options. After presenting a membership option the customer says:

Customer:

"Wow, I wasn't expecting that. You know at this time I really would rather think about it"

Sales Advisor:

"I totally understand. I say to a lot of my members that making a fitness decision isn't easy. In fact it could be stressful sometimes. I at least want to make sure that I know what it is that you are struggling with. Was it the initiation payment or the monthly dues with the option that I recommended?"

Customer:

"It was that money out of pocket for that initiation payment. I wasn't expecting that"

Sales Advisor:

"No worries, I totally get it. First I want to make sure that you are still pumped about losing 20 lbs. right"

Customer:

"Absolutely"

Sales Advisor:

"So why don't we do this. What if I told you that we have an option that has no initiation payment? Would that solve you problem?"

Customer:

"Yes that does"

The bottom line is that if or when a customer says no to purchasing a product or service, stop and think about how you would want to feel in that situation. Show some empathy because you should really understand where that customer is coming from. If you can do that then it is much easier to find a specific solution to their problem. Overcoming objections isn't about getting a person to say yes after they had just said no. It is about just getting a customer to re-consider. So what if you had the ability to have a customer re-consider his/her decision after having already said no sixty seconds prior. I think we would all sign up for that. That is what a business process or tool can do. It keeps you organized in your thoughts. The more organized your thoughts are, the more professional you sound and that is what business and sales are all about. Be a professional and you will go far.

The next time you go somewhere to purchase a product or service, I want you to really evaluate what kind of sales experience you had. What did you feel as the salesperson was taking you through the process. I bet that the more the salesperson made you feel comfortable, the greater the likelihood of you purchasing something from them. At the end of the day, people only buy if they believe in what they are buying.

CPSIA information can be obtained
at www.ICGtesting.com
Printed in the USA
FSHW01n1636160818
51422FS